The **10** Unbreakable **Rules** of Time Management

SAMER CHIDIAC

The 10 Unbreakable Rules of Time Management:
First Edition 2011

This title is also available in Audio & Electronic Book formats. For details and more of Samer Chidiac's Titles, visit: www.ChidiacBooks.com

Email: info@chidiacbooks.com

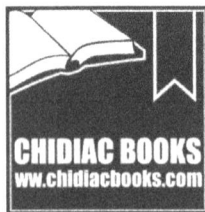

CHIDIAC BOOKS
ww.chidiacbooks.com

Copyright © 2011 Samer Chidiac
Published by ChidiacBooks.com

All rights reserved.

ISBN: 9953-0-2142-2
ISBN-13: 978-9953-0-2142-3

"If I spend my entire time devoted to their love…
all my life wouldn't be enough."

To Souad & Mokhtar,
My Parents.

CONTENTS

INTRODUCTION

I've learned from so many people and in different stages in my life that being the richest, the brightest or the most famous in the world does not matter when your time is up… What is left behind you is what you have done with your Time…

Procrastination is a term that became common not long ago. This is the first signal that you are slipping into poor time-management. Multi-tasking makes you assume that you are being more productive within the same given time; but this is a slippery slope. There is a thin line between the sufficient amount of worry that actually pushes you to fulfill your tasks, and the worry which may quickly transform into pressure that hinders your progress.

Our inability to fulfill our tasks "on time" stems from a common misconception; it's not that you "don't have time", but it is in fact you "don't appreciate the real value of YOUR TIME". You must realize that having POWER over YOUR TIME –and not the other way around- means that you have control over your life. And your valuable investment will pave the way to your success.

The Ten Unbreakable Rules of Time Management is unique in the sense that unlike other time-management manuals that may bombard you with theories, impracticalities and strategies inapplicable to your lifestyle, it is a very practical guide with immediate benefits.

This manual helps you develop a practical sense of time and hones your decision-making skills in order not to waste it. You will realize that you actually have more time on your hands than you think once you get organized. It may be easier than you think to direct your life towards the fulfillment of your goals if your full potentials are dedicated to them. Technology is one of these potentials and can greatly facilitate our lives when properly used.

In a nutshell, being successful does not make you manage your time well, but managing your time well will definitely make you successful.

By reading this book, you will understand the basic concepts of effective time management presented to you in simple language that sounds familiar.

I present you with the fruits of my extensive research across the different Best Practices in Time Management, as well as the long Experience and Successes of the most influential people that I have met in my life.

The 10 Unbreakable Rules of Time Management

RESPECT TIME

How Heavy is the Bottle of Water?

I once heard the story of a lecturer who was explaining stress management to his audience while holding a glass of water in his hand. I was inspired to try out his strategy in one of my time management workshops, so I held a bottle of water in the beginning of my session and started by asking: "How heavy is this bottle of water?"

The audience started reacting and each gave a different answer. Some tried a scientific approach saying that if 1L of water is equal to 1 kg and the bottle is ½ L and only half full, then it should be around 0.250 kg.

I smiled and replied back: "That would've been the correct answer if I was asking about the *weight* of the bottle of water. However, I asked how HEAVY the bottle of water is, and these are 2 different questions. If I hold the bottle of water for one minute, the weight would not be a problem. But maybe I won't feel *that* ok if I carried it for one hour. And if I keep on carrying it till the end of the workshop, I will be leaving the workshop in an ambulance! So, the actual weight of the bottle of water doesn't really matter. What really matters is *how long* I held it!"

Underestimating the Power of Time

We often estimate, over-estimate and under-estimate lots of activities using the exact same line of thought my audience had. In a survey we conducted, we asked the questions below to the audience who attended our Time Management courses and the following were

2

the answers of 90% of the respondents. Read on and judge for yourself.

What would you feel if:

		SUPERB	Indifferent	Not Cool	BAD
1.	Your heart stops				X
2.	You get a check for $ 1,000,000	X			
3.	A piece of delicious steak meat gets stuck between your teeth		X		
4.	You have to put your hand above a fire			X	

Thinking a little bit more about the above situations, you realize that your answer could change dramatically when you learn that:

1. When someone sneezes, people directly say "Bless you…" This is because medically speaking, that person's heart has stopped beating for a fraction of a second.
2. If you get a check for 1,000,000$ and held it for just 5 seconds before it was taken away from you, you actually had only 5 seconds of happiness and then it was all over.
3. If a piece of steak gets stuck between your teeth for more than 30 minutes, you will start feeling uncomfortable. If it stays for over 2 hours, you will lose all sense of concentration and won't be able to perform any task.
4. You can pass your hand quickly above a candle or a small fire, and this would not leave any sign of burn; in fact, you will barely feel the heat at all.

The conclusion from all this is that time can make virtually any theory possible, so you can make Time your best friend or your Worst enemy.

"Time waits for No Man. Yesterday is History; Tomorrow is Mystery; and Today is a Gift; that's why we call it the Present"

~Alice Morse Earle

The Past, Present and Future

People fear the unknown and keep on speculating about what would happen in the FUTURE. This is called "worrying". I remember a personal experience that would best illustrate this point.

"Due to my full schedule, I used to hit the gym at exactly 6:00 AM every day before I went to the office. I used to perform the same exercises for the same durations every single time. I would start with cycling, and then I would spend some time on the treadmill before I showered and left.

On one particular day, I arrived and noticed that out of the 10 cable TV screens on the walls of the gym, only 2 were functioning and the rest were powered off. The 2 working screens were right facing the bikes where I usually started my exercise. I spent the whole 20 minutes of cycling thinking about how boring my time on the treadmill was going to be with no TV screen. Funnily, by the time I finished cycling and reached the treadmill exercise, all the screens were actually functioning. So, I simply wasted my 20 minutes of cycling worrying about the "empty and boring" 45 minutes on the treadmill that never actually happened!"

People often "regret" something that has passed; they can't turn back time and go back to "do it right". They waste too much time on "regret mode" to the extent that they actually miss lots of good opportunities to have a good time.

On a different note, at around 1:15 AM and while we were both working late at Microsoft offices in Beirut, I had an interesting conversation about regret with Khaled Chebat, one of my mentors and good friends.

Khaled told me that there are only 2 things to do about the past:
- If you can do something about it, then go do it now.
- If you *can't*, regretting won't really help much.

Is Time Money or is it actually More Valuable?

Time is all around us; we all share the same 24 hours per day. Whatever you do would not extend those 24h for you, and no matter how *bad* these hours go, they won't ever shrink. But in fact, how you spend your time does make you who you are.

People don't deal with time as a commodity like they do with money. You can always make more money, but you can't get back the past 2 years of your life, nor can you buy an extra hour to live.

I felt inspired by Professor Randy Pauch who had cancer and spent the last few months of his life educating thousands on the value of realizing your dreams and managing your time…

Professor Pauch gave the example of students who come to him and ask him how much a master's degree is worth. He reflected on the differences between two groups: students who came in to discuss whether the degree is worth the money or not, and whom he would throw out of his office; and students with whom he would gladly spend all day, and who would tell him that they are not sure how they wanted to spend the next 2 years of their lives. The latter group is confused concerning whether to pursue a master's degree or not, but their dilemma is not the money at all. His special appreciation for the latter group is rooted in the fact that these students are discussing Time.

A person who values himself starts by valuing his time; so to start with, just think of how much you're worth? How much would you make per month in a steady job? Multiply that by 3 or 4, and then divide that by 160. This is how some consultants calculate their hourly fees. So if you make 1500$ / month, your hourly rate is almost 37.5$. So the Value of your time indicates how valuable you are.

"Value yourself and you become more important"

But there's more on that. In one of his sales seminars, Zig Ziglar, the legendary American motivational speaker, once said that insurance companies pay millions and millions of dollars every year for lost eyes, arms, broken legs etc. When you analyze it, you are physically worth millions of dollars. Mentally, experts estimated that if they invest billions of dollars to duplicate your brain, it would take a computer the size of the empire state building, and it would still not do what your brain can do every second of every day: generate a thought.

You become more important when you first realize how valuable you are; you become more valuable in your organization when you put more experience on the table.

They say that experience comes with Time, and there are NO shortcuts to getting it. This is just like the example that one woman needs 9 months to deliver her baby, but 9 women can't deliver a baby in one month.

"Good Judgment comes from Experience and experience comes from lots of Bad Judgments"

Finally, there is an example on this same point that I always give in the sales excellence trainings I deliver. I ask the sales persons before me: "Consider this task. You have to deliver a 15 minutes presentation to a TOP potential customer; and if the result is positive, you would win a $ 150,000 deal. Then what's the worth of your 15 minutes? The answer is 150k, and *every minute* is worth $ 10,000 even if you don't say a word during this minute. So, when you think about it this way, you will cut the none-sense and make every word count!"

Time vs. Timing

Although TIME in itself is the subject in this rule, its derivation *"timing"* is just as important.

The expressions "Too soon" , "Too late", "Pre-mature"… give the impression that the task was fulfilled but not ON TIME.

Many religions elaborate on the importance of Time, putting Time in the practical form of Timing. For instance, some prayers have to be done at specific timings; fasting is also done at specific times of the year and according to set timings when you fast and break your fast.

Moreover, *good timing* and *bad timing* play a major role in public speaking; the speaker has to carefully choose the timing of his words, especially punch words. Also, he/she has to be careful when to change the tone of their voice to keep the audience engaged, attentive and interested.

RULE #1 IN A NUTSHELL

RESPECT TIME

The essence of this first rule is the word *respect*; when you respect time and respect your time, everything around you will start to change in the right direction. If you try to go around time and take shortcuts at the expense of your time, you are acting just like a thief who would take the easy way out by stealing money instead of working hard to make it. It's just like a voided check.

So respect time! It is all what we have, and you may wake up one day and realize that you have... *LESS.*

DECIDE

I was listening to one of Jim Rohn's seminars about leadership and I quote the following:

"The Miracle of Believing is Individual... Is singular.. I wish I could believe for all of you, but the truth remains that you need to believe for yourself..."

I would simply replace the word "Believe" with the expression "Decide to believe", and I would also emphasize the word DECIDE. If you could decide for someone else, there wouldn't be any wars, any divorces, any problems between individuals or even countries... The fact remains that you can't decide for someone else.

My favorite saying by Galileo Galilei (the man who invented the telescope) is:

"You can't teach a man anything; you can only help him discover it within himself..."

This saying means a lot to me because I believe that you simply can't change people; people can change on their own if they decide to do so. Yet, many people still refuse to believe that the power of change lies within themselves. If you don't decide to change, no method, procedure or person would have any impact whatsoever on your life.

Implicit Decisions

In the course of my research for my other books, the "Work Love Balance" Series, I spent a considerable period of time building an understanding of what we can call: Implicit Decisions.

When two strangers meet for the first time, no matter where or how, there's the simple truth that one or both of them will directly and implicitly decide to either accept or reject the relationship, even before a single word is said.

It is undeniably simple and true; we use implicit decisions more than explicit ones. Here, it is important to note that saying an implicit decision out loud does not make it an explicit decision. Making an actual decision and acting upon it does.

For instance, the use of verbs is important. I often hear people saying: "I can't seem to *FIND* time to do anything"; so the last time one of my clients used this expression, I smiled and said,

"You MAKE time by DECIDING NOT TO DO SOMETHING ELSE"

This also applies to changing habits. For instance, if you're a junk food lover and you want to change your eating habits, you do not actually stop eating altogether; you rather eat healthy food.

So the secret is all within you…

The Secret is in your Mind

Our biggest fears come from what we don't know. In 2011, when I was in an "entrepreneurs mentoring boot camp" done by the Mowgli Foundation in Lebanon, I developed a deeper understanding about the same concept: it's not just what you don't know that's scary; what is really scary is what you don't know that you don't know.

Taking a decision can be challenging depending on its effects. Worrying about taking the decision before you do it lies in the fact you wouldn't know whether you made the right or the wrong decision until after the decision has already been made.

But fearing the unknown is perfectly NORMAL and shouldn't keep you from living your life and taking decisions that would influence you and your world. What I want to emphasize here is that what you think *defines you*, and it even *CONTROLS* you.

Yes, our thoughts control us. After my extensive research in psychology, I've seen this probably everywhere: *"You Become what you Think of yourself"*

And decisions come from within you. Now you may say that we make decisions every day, at the end of each of our meetings for example. But despite the fact that we are making decisions, we are still not moving forward.

VOILA!

To make a REAL decision is to decide to COMMIT to that decision, whatever it was.

Let me ask you this: do you know someone who still lives in the past, or someone who didn't get over a certain incident, relationship, etc? Do you feel the impact of that particular thought on that person's life? So you see where I'm going here…

It's plain simple, yet it's very delicate. Deciding gives you great powers; and the more you practice decision-making, the more likely you are to improve in your career. Moreover, the more important you become in your organization, the more you will need to make more important decisions.

And with experience you will make better decisions every time.

"All what we are is the result of all that we have thought"

~ *Buddha*

D for Decide

Here are your "Go-To"s from this rule:

- Decide to let go and decide to move on
- Decide to drop limiting beliefs
- Decide to think positively
- Decide to DELEGATE
- Decide to DO IT!
- Decide & do it with authority and responsibility

There's a common term in time-management about decision-making, and it's called the 4Ds: Drop it, Delay it, Delegate it or Do it.

So, every time you face a new situation that requires a decision, I recommend that you take a look and use Stephen Covey's Epic method: (The Urgent/ Important Diagram from the Book <u>The 7 Habits of Highly Effective People</u>)

Important but Not Urgent	Important and Urgent
Planning, researching, design, development, creativity…	Emergencies, planned tasks, commitments, meetings…
Not Important, not Urgent	Not Important but Urgent
Gossip / chats…	Interruptions (Phone, visitors…), Trivial tasks, internet chatting, updates on Facebook…

After practicing writing things down for a while, that method will be programmed in your mind, so your decisions will be made instinctively and on the fly.

Here are few more tips before ending this rule.

Do the UGLY work yourself, and delegate for other tasks. Give people tasks based on their capacities in order to avoid under-estimating or over-estimating delegates. And finally don't *procrastinate*. Some people say, "If I wait enough, then probably I won't have to do it."

RULE #2 IN A NUTSHELL

DECIDE

Deciding can be easy, but committing to your decisions is what actually matters.

Viewing life as a series of decisions would make you realize how important every action you have taken and will take in the future is; so, start getting used to making better decisions and always go back and reflect on these decisions to see what went wrong and what you would change the next time you need to make similar ones.

And don't under-estimate the small details you can decide on or change in your life. As Walid Abu-Hadba, Corporate Vice President at Microsoft once told me: "The difference between success and failure is details; details are like the Fine Print… You sometimes need to decide on them first".

RE-DEFINE YOUR FREE TIME

When you often hear the word FREE, you automatically associate it with money, and particularly money that you don't have to pay. So for example, if you get a free soft-drink with your meal, you consider the soft-drink as something paid for by the restaurant.

So an implicit conclusion from your perception of the word FREE is that it's not something that doesn't have a certain value, but it's rather something that is paid for by someone else.

Based on the same analogy, let me associate this with time. You frequently hear the expression "Free Time", and normally you just feel better when you hear it. We understand "free time" as an empty slot of time that we can either fill with something or rather do nothing at all. (Where I come from, "FREE time" translates to "EMPTY time" or a "Time for Emptiness", which I find a little annoying).

Finding the right definition

If you agree with what you have just read above, I assume you haven't read Rule #2 where I explained about the reality of the verb Find in "Finding Time".

"You Can't FIND time; you just need to decide NOT to do something Else"

Interesting? So from now on, our 1st definition would be:
"Free-time is a time that was originally committed to doing something that we eventually decided not to do"

That definition alone wouldn't make our life easier, but it's a good start. Rule #3 is about changing that definition so we can make better use of our time. Let me give you an example.

You were at a gas station, and let's say you needed 10 minutes to fill the tank. After it was filled, you threw away some garbage and went into the gas station's store to buy some stuff. Performing all of these actions in that *order*, you ended up spending 20 minutes at the gas station.

Let us change few sentences from the example above in the following manner.

You were at a gas station, and let's say you needed 10 minutes to fill the tank. While the tank was being filled, you threw away some garbage and went into the gas station's store to buy some stuff. Performing all of those actions simultaneously, you ended up spending 10 minutes at the gas station.

Now what just happened? I only replaced "and after that" and "then" with the word "While". This way, you saved 50% of your time at the gas station.

The word "WHILE" is not a curse but it's a blessing. Apparently, you can finish lots of tasks WHILE you are doing others.

Now you may think a little and say: "But that's called multi-tasking, which I have already heard of long ago. You didn't come up with anything new".

Well "multi-tasking" is dividing your energy among multiple tasks. So while your computer can be reading and writing files simultaneously, you can't be reading a book and a newspaper and writing an article at the same time.

So the difference between multi-tasking and the leverage of free/committed time is simply the awareness of the context and not having to divide your resources.

So I would re-define my first definition in the following manner:

"Free-time is ANY time that IS originally committed to actually doing something else"

"All that really Belongs to us is time; even he who has nothing else has that"

~ Baltasar Gracian

Your Extended Free-Time

To make this work to your advantage, you have to simply check the *context* of your committed time-slots in order to decide what else can be done WHILE your task is being done.

The following examples illustrate my idea.

- You can Exercise WHILE you Watch TV / DVD.
- You can perform many tasks like reading your Newspaper / Book / Magazine, or finishing some administrative tasks like your expense reports on your laptop, WHILE traveling on the train or plane, or WHILE you are waiting to board.
- You can check/reply to emails via your phone WHILE waiting in the queue at the Bank. (Yes, some emails require less than 5 minutes to reply to.)
- You can listen to audio books WHILE you are driving. (I have a friend who actually learned FRENCH that very same way.)
- If you have a 40-minute drive, schedule some calls to make WHILE you are driving or waiting in traffic. (Make sure to take all the necessary precautions and tools like Hands-Free / Car-Kit)
- Schedule some meetings with clients and colleagues at breakfast, lunch or dinner so you can talk WHILE eating.
- If you're doing a computer task that requires a long time to process (such as generating a big report, or copying large files etc…), you can perform another non-computer related task WHILE you are waiting.

When applied correctly, this rule can increase your productivity. It can also increase your "customer satisfaction" because you will be perceived as "respecting of others' time".

A final example about this: if you were a cashier at a Supermarket, customers usually line up waiting for you to serve them; applying the same example of the gas station, you can take a look at the queue and make some adjustments. For instance, WHILE the first customer is un-loading his/her cart, you can recommend that another customer with very few items pass through. You can redirect some customers to other less busy cashiers.

I once accompanied a friend to the bank; he wanted to check a very simple matter about his credit card. The "queue" was made up of just us and another customer. We reached the bank 20 minutes before it stopped receiving customers.

Funnily, the one single other customer took a lot of time for his service to be completed. He was signing papers and organizing them while we waited, and while our task would have taken no more than two minutes. As you may have guessed, we ended up waiting for 30 minutes until another clerk in this bank passed by and offered to help us. Also as expected, our task took exactly 4 minutes to be completed.

We thanked the clerk who offered to help, while neither the teller nor the customer actually bothered.

My friend then decided to move his account to another bank. Moreover, each of us shared this bank experience with several people. Such small incidents greatly influence the reputation of corporations and organizations.

RULE #3 IN A NUTSHELL

RE-DEFINE YOUR FREE TIME

Inspired by John Adair who stressed the importance of free/committed time in his books on management & leadership, this rule is not only about free time itself. It is about your *Awareness* of what free time means from now on. You will realize how many MORE things can be done in your free time, things that you didn't think about before. The key here is simply –as much as possible- to *plan* well and in advance.

And when you become aware about something, you start realizing how common that "something" is. Upon buying a new car, have you ever felt directly the next day that everyone is driving the same model?

GET ORGANIZED

Reading from several books about managing people, I've always found a very common sentence: "Make sure the employee has everything he needs to be able to perform his tasks right".

It's true. If you don't have all the necessary resources for you to do your job properly, chances are that you're going to "suffer". But sometimes, you do have everything you need to do your job well, but due to lack of organization, you don't.

This rule seems the most obvious among all, yet you find lots of people continuously saying: "I'm not the type of persons who is organized". It is true that being unorganized may not have any dangerous results; but definitely being more organized would render much greater results.

Organize your workspace

Most employees spend over 55% of their time a year in their offices. So for those, spending 8 hours per day working out of the desk is an integral part of their daily lives. How organized this desk is reflects how organized they are and how productive they will be.

Question: Do you know how much time a year we spend "trying to find things"?
Answer: "Pretty much!"

Now sometimes, your desk says to you: *"I OWN YOU… I have more things than you can do".*

Just like you would enjoy driving your car more when it's CLEAN and working properly, you will enjoy working in your clean and organized environment.

The first thing you need to do here is to create a *reference system*, a system which enables you to know where everything should be. Saying "I always place that stuff here" or "I know where they are" is always better than running around and saying "WHERE IS IT?"

I personally recommend a *physical inbox*, which is a small box where you put everything that you haven't processed yet. You can then gradually process and place items and always *KNOW* where they are.

If you don't have a *double monitor* for your computer or laptop, getting one would definitely give you more productivity. For instance, you can leave your email open on one screen and finish your actual work on the other. You won't believe the amount of productivity you can get then.

Organize your Interruptions

Two out of each three persons I coached were convinced that their time-management system was almost flawless. The single exception or problem that hindered their productivity was their inability to properly manage interruptions.

I never agreed with the first statement (the flawless system), but I always agree that most people are incapable of managing interruptions.

Question: "Do you know how many times an average person gets interrupted per day?"
Answer: "TOO MUCH!!"

NEVER mistake being "nice" to someone with accepting their interruption whenever it happens.

If someone passes uninvited by your desk and talks to you for few minutes, that sounds innocent and ok. But that still counts as an interruption.

Interruptions take around 6-7 minutes to happen, but they take a LOT more to recover from. So, if you're writing software for example and you get 5 – 6 interruptions, that's seriously BAD.

Unless you lock yourself in a room, you just can't avoid interruptions from happening. But here are some interesting tips on managing interruptions (from professor Pauch):

- Make your office comfortable for you and *optionally* comfortable for others.
- Stand up when someone arrives.
- Bound the amount of time (say something like: I only have 5 minutes. This way you'll have the privilege to extend if you want to.
- If they *don't get it*, walk with them to the door.
- If they still didn't get it, just leave them and walk out.

Organize your Calls

It's part of our day-to-day duties to talk on the phone, to make and receive calls. But it's important to distinguish between the calls that are planned and those which are not.

Planned calls are simply those that you are expecting. If you are expecting a call at 10 AM to discuss a specific project, all you have to do is make sure that your call doesn't drift away from its original purpose. You also have to make sure that it doesn't drag beyond the 45 minutes that were allotted to it.

Unplanned calls are the ones that just pop up unexpectedly. Even if you are the one who is making the call (rather than the one receiving it), this doesn't prevent your time from being wasted.

First, I would recommend that you buy a speakerphone or a headset (if you do not already have one). This way, you will have both hands free to write or take care of other things in the meantime.

Second and here's an interesting tip:

STAND UP WHILE YOU TAKE YOUR CALLS. This way you are more likely to keep the call brief and straight to the point and to end it promptly.

Third, have something interesting to do after you have finished your call.

If you're the one calling, start by announcing the objectives of the call,
"Hi X I'm calling to talk to you about A, B & C…. and then about A, B & C".

Make your calls before lunch or right before the end of the day. This way, no matter how interesting you think you are, the receiver is more likely to have more important things to do such as to have a meal or leave the office.

As for Tele-Marketers who keep calling to sell you something or to convince you to help some association by donating money or buying some un-necessary goods, you should have a brave-heart and just hang up while you're talking to them.

And finally, I recommend that you use my method:

My method is simple: *I turn phone calls into e-mails*. So, if I'm not expecting the call or I don't know the caller, I simply don't answer. I have shared that strategy with everyone I know saying, "it's not personal, but I don't answer my phone. If you need something from me, email me or text-message me." It is recommended to have two separate phone numbers: a professional one with which to share with people, and a personal one restricted to your closed circle.

There is nothing more unproductive (for both caller and receiver) than to call at a bad time. It's even worse when you call at a bad time and expect the receiver to take down notes or tasks. Have you ever received a call while you're in a meeting and you had to keep a mental note that you later on forgot?

"A small leak can sink a great ship"
"A place for everything, everything in its place"
~ Benjamin Franklin

Organize your meetings

Meetings can be time-savers or time-wasters depending on how well they were conducted.

During lots of meetings, you find several attendees working on their Blackberry, replying to emails, or doing anything else while the meeting is in session. If you seriously want a meeting to be productive, lock the room door, unplug the phone…
If the meeting is not worth your time, then it's not worth attending in the first place.

There should always be an agenda for the meeting, and at the end of the meeting, someone should write minutes of what happened and a list of responsibilities assigned to each person or department. These minutes and lists should be mailed to all involved parties. This way, you won't show up the week after without clear expectations.

I was asking Joe Wilson, a Senior director at Microsoft, about some of his tips on time management. He had lots of very valuable ones, two of which are very relevant to this rule:

1- Meetings shouldn't take more than 30 minutes; If you cut the "Hey how you doin'? How's family? What's up with the Barcelona vs. Real Madrid game?", and stick to the agenda of the meeting, 30 minutes should be more than enough.
2- If you have a meeting with someone, you go to their office, and not the other way around; this way, you control what time you leave.

Organize your life using a System

USE a *system*! It doesn't matter whether it's a sophisticated electronic calendar or a simple fridge calendar, but there SHOULD be a system that tells you where you need to be next Thursday at 2 PM!

Learn to do Everything ONCE! This way, you don't *re-invent* the wheel. For instance, touch every piece of paper only ONCE. This is very true and essential for emails.

Keep close track of the time to know where and how are you spending your time (and you're ALWAYS spending more than you think).

I would personally go with having a technological device to help you organize yourself. It is important to pay attention to the fact that the device doesn't make your system work; YOU make it work by using it effectively.

Some people consider that their email inbox is their to-do list, which is not true. You should have a separate to-do list with the tasks spread out according to the time slots you assign.

RULE #4 IN A NUTSHELL

GET ORGANIZED

When we say *get organized*, we do not only mean manage your appearance and clean your desk! Getting organized is much more than that.

- The way you do things needs to be organized.
- The way you deal with people needs to be organized.
- The way you process your papers needs to be organized.
- The way you talk on the phone needs to be organized.
- The way you do meetings needs to be organized.
- The way you deal with interruptions needs to be organized.
- The way you process your emails needs to be organized.

And that won't happen if you don't have a system in place.

So finally,

It's all about getting organized physically, mentally, socially and corporately.

KNOW WHERE YOU'RE GOING & WHY

Over the past 10 years, I have literally interviewed thousands of people from all over the world. These people were candidates to work for me in one of my companies, clients, partners, or people I coached on different occasions. One of the most common questions that I would consider the "Hello" of my interviewing dictionary was:

"Where do you see yourself 5 to 10 years from now?"

Around 80% of interviewees didn't know the answer to that question despite the fact that they have been repeatedly asked this question in possibly every job interview they have had.

My question was intended to ask someone to *foresee* their future; I rather used this question for ME to *see* their future.

Walt Disney once said: "if you can dream it, you can do it!". I can't emphasize enough the power of your dreams; that power is the first step towards any accomplishment.

So when you close your eyes and dream about something, you can see it… And once you could see it, you can achieve it…

Some of the most successful people I've met always told me that they could visualize their life and their successes ahead. If they had a dream house in mind, they knew exactly what this dream house looks like: How many rooms it had; its location; the color of the walls… If they had a dream car in mind, they knew exactly which model. They could close their eyes and smell the inside of that car.

No Plans = You're Wasting your Time

I remember the following quote by the famous Boxer, Muhammad Ali Clay, "The man who views the world at 50 the same as he did when he was 20 has wasted 30 years of his life"

Time flies! You can watch 10 years of your life pass you by with very little notable achievements; you feel really bad when you start comparing your "successes" to those of others. The real person you should compare your success to is You!

I once wrote an article about success, and among the many definitions of success, there is one that I consider to be very true yet not very common:

"a successful person is a person who lives his life the way he wanted"

Now that's a very powerful statement because it's not measured by power, money, fame, etc… It's just plain simple: Real success is not accidental. This brings me to the core of Rule #5.

Roughly, and in very simple terms, if you want something to happen, you need to know what it is that you want to happen, when you need it to happen (even if it's in 10 years), what you need to make it happen, the parties involved for it to happen, any foreseen obstacles that would stop it from happening…That is actually called PLANING!

Winston Churchill once said: "Failing to plan is planning to fail". So guess what? You're actually doing it! You're actually planning! All you need to do now is to plan in the right direction. You can make up for bad talent by planning…

"Failing to plan, is planning to fail"

~ Winston Churchill

Setting Goals & Objectives

The first step in planning in the right direction is to set goals & objectives for your life. Now there are 7 different kinds of Goals (in no particular order):
1- Physical
2- Financial
3- Spiritual
4- Career
5- Family
6- Mental
7- Social

Setting these goals has to create CHANGE to be effective, like Zig Ziglar once said: "Thinking big creates the excitement necessary for accomplishment."

To do so, you can start by asking yourself this:

What do I REALLY Want…?

And again I stress on the word REALLY, because *really* is not based on the *reality* of your dreams, and certainly it's not based on what's available now or can be accomplished now. Remember that the entire world WILL change 10 years from now, but chances are that your dreams won't.

Let me give you this example. In my coaching sessions, I always discuss career development. Many years ago, the term *social media* didn't exist, and interacting with people online was something specific to "online dating" (Although this is a very common term, I think that the term is misleading because you can't DATE online at all; you just search, email and IM.) and making virtual friends etc… Most corporations of different sizes didn't find the necessity to incorporate *online socializing* into their plans. One in every 500 companies had a position (or a shared duty) in their structure for an "Online Reputation Manager". But with the evolution of the web to web 2.0, and after the huge impact of websites like Facebook, Twitter & YouTube on our daily communication and interactions, 1 in every

5 companies around the world nowadays has the Digital / Social media strategy incorporated in their plans.

What does that mean? It means that if in 2006 you had a passion to interact with people online and everyone else thought that you're wasting your time, then in 2010 you could work in a very reputable company as a "Social Media Strategist", making 2 times what you were making before and doing the thing you've always had a passion for!

To establish the "Where" are you going, you can start by throwing a few "Why"s here and there.

Ask yourself "WHY am I doing this?"; "WHY am I NOT doing it?"

In some 1:1 meetings with my employees, I ask them this funny question (especially coming from me)

"Why are you doing this? Why are you working in this company as an Operations manager or Graphic designer or IT… etc?"

With experience, managers could easily spot when an employee loses his/her spark doing their work. So the right answer should always be "I enjoy spending time making creative designs, managing deadlines, working with numbers… etc"

If it's not fun… then why do it?

In the process of asking yourself the *why* question, you will start mixing between Professional & Personal

- Where: is more related to your *Professional* life
- Why: is more *Personal* (we'll elaborate more on that later on in this rule)

The Why can impact the HOW; I'm sure you've heard the quote: *"When there's a will there's a way"*…

In this rule, I don't focus on the HOW; I only focus on the Where and the Why…

An example from the famous book <u>THE SECRET</u> would do the job of shifting your attention from the HOW to the Where/Why:

You can drive 20 miles A to point B and still reach your destination despite the fact that you can only see 20 meters ahead of you in the darkness using your car lights.

So setting your objectives and goals is "Where" you're going; the resulting achievement is the "Why".

In one of the 1:1 sessions I've had with Nasseem Tuffaha, who was a Senior Director in Microsoft back then, I asked for some advice on changing positions within Microsoft. He asked me this simple yet very powerful question:

"What position do you want to reach after the next one?"

We had a very interesting talk back then, but the essence of that talk was that Nasseem explained to me how my next position should pave the way to the one that comes after. So, I may be going into a very uninteresting or difficult role, but that should be necessary to where I'm heading.

Go S.M.A.R.T.E.R

You need to set LONG term goals. This way, the SHORT term frustrations won't stop you. Occasionally, circumstances beyond your control do arise ("things happen") such as market change, family problems, accidents, sickness etc... That can be seriously intimidating.

Your goals need to be S.M.A.R.T and even S.M.A.R.T.E.R

S.pecific
M.easurable
A.greed
R.ealistic
T.ime-bounded

E.valuated
R.eviewed

There are many online books and articles on methods to setting S.M.A.R.T & S.M.A.R.T.E.R goals. I recommend that you take a look at some to help you properly set your objectives and goals (John Adair's *Handbook of Management and Leadership* for instance).

Once your goals are set on the different areas of your life, you can start planning and changing your plans accordingly. Remember: you can't change plans that you don't HAVE.

When I started applying this thinking, lots of things started making more sense to me. Lots of opportunities have arisen before me that I didn't intentionally take advantage of, simply because they didn't or wouldn't contribute to my long term objectives. I keep reminding myself of what I once read about logical thinking: "When you're climbing a tree and your aim is to reach to the top, sometimes the leaves with the *fruits* may not be on the way to the top. They may either distract you or change your path altogether."

One of the mistakes I find lots of people - including some high rank Managers- making is that they believe that they need to do EVERYTHING by themselves. And the word *delegate* is totally inexistent to them.

We've talked about delegation in Rule#2; however, one tip in this domain is that if you want to delegate, you should focus on the WHERE / WHY than on the HOW.

The Real WHY

There are lots of justifications that we come up with to explain our lives, and we link things from here and there in order to *justify* these *justifications*.

I constantly ask the people I coach on time-management about why they want to be more efficient. Most of them reply, "to make MORE money". When I ask why, they always reply, "to be able to live better". And when I dig deeper with my "why"s, they say that they want to live happier lives with their loved ones. Then, I rest my case.

The expression "Work Life Balance" existed in the first place because people are working harder every day, and not being able to come back on time to their homes to see the people that matter the most to them.

I am in no way lecturing about the standards of your life. I only want to draw your attention that in order to HONOR your "Why", you need to be both *Effective* & *Efficient* at your work so you finish things on time.

What's the difference? What did I just say? *Both* Effective & Efficient?

If you want an easier way to memorize the difference, remember this sentence: *"Being effective is about doing the right things, while being efficient is about doing the things in the right manner."*

Compare the following: An employee in a company who works for ten hours every day, stays overtime, and is always delayed, and another more successful worker in the same position who finishes the same amount of work in six hours.

In this example, the employee working 10 hours/day can be very efficient in his work, doing things as he's supposed to do. But his colleague is doing the *Right* things in the *Right* manner, so he's not wasting time on things that are unproductive or ineffective as he accomplishes his work goals.

And always remember WHY you take a vacation, because it's NOT a vacation if you're working...

RULE #5 IN A NUTSHELL

KNOW WHERE YOU'RE GOING AND WHY

Just remember this saying by Dr. Covey:

"How many on their death Beds wished they had spent more time at the office or Watching TV?"

Basically the answer is: NO ONE. They think about their loved ones, their families and those they have served.

That's why you should always be true to yourself; answer this individualistic WHERE Question, and always remember the *true* WHY.

STOP USING YOUR HEAD

T his is the most important rule, and applying it would impact your life immediately!

I can't stress enough on the importance of Rule #6; if this book were a restaurant menu, then this rule is the item *"most Recommended by the Chef"*.

How we use our Heads

Interestingly, we have amazing abilities to lie to our brains. I have spent a considerable amount of time studying & researching how our brain functions and what its great POWERS are.

And I am continuously and repeatedly amazed by what I find out, especially when it comes to the power of your sub-conscious mind in particular.

"Do you know that your subconscious mind can compute 2,000,000 thought/second? Amazing fact, isn't it?"

So all of your experiences, thoughts, memories, knowledge, feelings since you were born are registered in your brain (somewhere), and every time you want to perform ANYTHING, you get the answer from the INSIDE; then you just do it or don't do it.

So, if you're an experienced manager, and one of your employees drops by and tells you about an emergency that requires your immediate attention, you are asked to DECIDE (Check Rule #2) on what to do. Automatically, you start suggesting this and that, you talk to this person and that, and you perform certain actions almost without thinking…

Now where did that came from? It simply came from your subconscious that is computing and cross referencing all of what happened in your life, and pushing the answer back to you.

But guess what? Most people can't benefit much from this amazing natural HUMAN ability simply because they can't realize that their heads are LOADED with 100s of *other-non-related-things*. These things occupy their mind and oblige them to think using whatever is left from their available 'head' in order to make a decision.

Examples we take for granted

Allow me to give you many facts related to this rule.

I have sat once with my executive assistant, Maryam, who was getting married few months later. She was asking me to help her "organize her thoughts" and create a system for her to keep track of and execute the to-do list for her wedding.

Regardless of what part of the world you come from, and regardless of whether the wedding is big or small, for any bride, this is BIG and *stress* is written all over it.

So I started asking her questions and writing things down: from the invitees list, to the theme and location, to catering to the wedding dress etc.. Then I went deeper into each item, and then even deeper into each Task related to each sub-item, and finally their dependencies.

After 3 hours, around 8-9 pages and almost 100 bullet points of OBVIOUS To-Do tasks, we finished the meeting. But what is worth mentioning is that she wasn't aware of the existence of at least 40% of these items. Moreover, she agreed that 99% of all of these items were haunting her thoughts and causing a lot of stress MONTHS before the wedding. Also, whether she admitted it or not, it was definitely AFFECTING almost everything else she was doing in her life including work.

I can give 100s of similar examples. Now, brace yourself and read the following:

1- Each friend of yours has: a birthday, relationship, work status, family, hobbies…etc. You have to remember his company's name, date of birth, name of domestic partner, names of children, hobbies, favorite food, dislikes…

2- Your Spouse/husband / GF / BF / Lover: Date of your first meeting, location, details, anniversaries, family details, food preferences, hobbies, name of siblings, names of friends, favorite music, favorite movie… etc. (and I bet that this list would go on and on and on…)

3- Your Car and all of the related features and information: maintenance, history, features…

4- Your Home/Household (Chores, Plumbing, electric, landlord, walls/floors/ceilings, appliances, kitchen appliances…)

5- Upcoming events (Special occasions, birthdays, anniversary, weddings, graduations, holidays, travel / vacations, social events, Sporting event…)

6- Commitments / promises to (Children, spouse, family, friends, Borrowed Items...)

7- Hobbies, Books, Records, CDs, DVDs

8- Errands: (Supermarket, Bank, Cleaner, pharmacy,…)

9- Community / Spirituals

10- Bills, personal finances, Banks…

…And I haven't Even got to ANYTHING related to Studies or Work.

So I know that you get the message of how much your head is currently loaded.

I don't know about you, but I simply don't have enough BRAIN to spare on things that I can use paper or any system to host them at.

"Plant the seed of desire in your mind and it forms a nucleus with power to attract to itself everything needed for fulfillment…"

~ Robert Collier

Your Head is Not a Collection Point

In her Book *"Taking back your life using Outlook 2007"*, Sally Mcghee, an expert on productivity, explained so much about how to clear your mind and how not to use your mind as a *collection point*. The same concept applies to the laws of productivity presented by David Allen in *"Getting things Done"* while leveraging Microsoft Outlook. (That book changed my life and I highly recommend it.)

It's important to note that we collect To-Do items every day from almost everywhere: from emails, voice mails, phone chats and meetings to personal chats and projects etc…

But what would happen if you used your head as a collection point?

Being single and living alone for years, remembering even the smallest thing such as buying shampoo was a challenge for me with the very busy life I had.

So, while taking a shower, I keep on telling myself that I needed to buy a new bottle of shampoo. Funnily, even when I pass by the Shampoo isle in the supermarket, I always FORGET to get one.

But in all cases, the un-finished "buying a shampoo" task stayed in my head, and kept on haunting from time to time no matter where I was. Sometimes I am delivering a speech and I notice someone with nice hair, and something from deep inside would *JUMP* and say: "SHAMPOO!!"

Hence, this small and almost meaningless task stays in our heads, and so do 100s of similar things. We think that they are not worth putting them anywhere else, so we keep them in our HEAD.

RESULT

The result of all what you have read before can be summarized in one question.

How many times have you found yourself taking significantly more TIME to finish a 10-minute task? And once you've finished it, you say to yourself, "that wasn't that bad, so why didn't I finish it quicker?"

Coming from a technical background, I will ask you to think of your brain as your computer resource; the more you free it, the more of it you have to use on execution.

So keep your mind clear by leveraging the minimum of CONTROLLABLE collection points (Check Rule #4), and meditate from time to time by trying not to THINK of anything for a minute or 2 every day.

RULE #6 IN A NUTSHELL

STOP USING YOUR HEAD

Take some time and reflect on what may reside in your head as of now, and bring a piece of paper and un-load what's on your mind. You will be surprised with the results.

Start realizing that your brain is one of your biggest assets. When the capacity of your brain is fragmented on several issues, you are wasting the resources in your brain necessary for you to fulfill the task. It's like having a hundred dollars but being unable to use it except one penny at a time.

So please remember this,

Your Head is NOT a Collection point, so STOP USING it as one!

ACT AS IF

The Glass Jar: Rocks, Pebbles, Sand, and Water

I've heard this story (and lots of similar versions of it) when I was younger. It goes like this:

One day, an old professor in the School of Public Management in France was invited to lecture on the topic of "Efficient Time Management" in front of a group of 15 executive managers representing the largest, most successful companies in America. The lecture was one in a series of 5 lectures conducted in one day, and the old professor was given 1h to lecture.

Standing in front of this group of elite managers who were willing to write down every word that would come out of the famous professor's mouth, the professor slowly met eyes with each manager, one by one, and finally said, "we are going to conduct an experiment".

From under the table that stood between the professor and the listeners, the professor pulled out a big glass jar and gently placed it in front of him.

Next, he pulled out from under the table a bag of stones, each the size of a tennis ball, and placed the stones one by one in the jar. He did so until there was no room to add another stone in the jar. Lifting his gaze to the managers, the professor asked, "Is the jar full?" The managers replied, "Yes".

The professor paused for a moment, and replied, "Really?"

Once again, he reached under the table and pulled out a bag full of pebbles. Carefully, the professor poured the pebbles in and slightly rattled the jar, allowing the pebbles to slip through the larger stones, until they settled at the bottom. Again, the professor lifted his gaze to his audience and asked, "Is the jar full?"

At this point, the managers began to understand his intentions. One replied, "apparently not!"

"Correct", replied the old professor, now pulling out a bag of sand from under the table. Cautiously, the professor poured the sand into the jar. The sand filled up the spaces between the stones and the pebbles.

Yet again, the professor asked, "Is the jar full?"

Without hesitation, the entire group of students replied in unison, "NO!"

"Correct", replied the professor. And as was expected by the students, the professor reached for the pitcher of water that was on the table, and poured water in the jar until it was absolutely full. The professor now lifted his gaze once again and asked, "What great truth can we surmise from this experiment?"

With his thoughts on the lecture topic, one manager quickly replied, *"We learn that as full as our schedules may appear, if we only increase our effort, it is always possible to add more meetings and tasks."*

"No", replied the professor. The great truth that we can conclude from this experiment is:

If we don't put all the larger stones in the jar first, we will never be able to fit all of them later.

The auditorium fell silent, as every manager processed the significance of the professor's words in their entirety.

The old professor continued, "What are the large stones in your life? Health? Family? Friends? Your goals? Doing what you love? Fighting for a Cause? Taking time for yourself?"

What we must remember is that it is most important to attend to the lager stones in our lives, because if we don't do so, we are likely to miss out on life altogether. If we give priority to the smaller things in life (pebbles & sand), our lives will be filled up with less important things, leaving little or no time or room for the things in our lives that are most important to us…

And the story continued with the old professor explaining which represented what, and went deeper in his explanations until he finished his lecture with a big applause from his audience.

Although Rule #5 (Know where you're going and why) is all about identifying your *stones*, your *pebbles* and *sands* etc, this rule is all about how you PLACE them in the right order, or in other terms: *How to Prioritize!*

Prioritizing is usually a characteristic of highly experienced people; the more experienced you are, the better you are at prioritizing because we always have too many things to do, with little time to do them. So the truth is that we WON'T be able to do them all, but we can do our priorities.

"*We know what we've lost when it's gone…*"

~ The Scorpions

Act as If

Although the introduction of this rule is more on the importance of prioritization, the essence of it is about Acting upon the prioritization.

Don't suppose; ACT AS IF:

- Your deadline is tomorrow. (create a fake deadline)
- You're getting married tomorrow (supposing you're single) and going on a leave for 2 months.
- The task does not belong to you but to one of your loved ones.
- You're the CEO of the company.
- You only have 1 month to live.
- You have already finished the task. (you can see what happens if the task is not fulfilled)
- Your Goal is only a portion of the original one.
- You're based in a different country and you're only visiting here for few days.

Loads of examples and explanations are to be extracted here, because doing things at the last minute is really costly. So for instance, if you put yourself in a mindset AS IF you're taking a leave for 2 months starting tomorrow, automatically the level of priority for lots of tasks would change. If you only have 1 month to live, lots of "important" things that occupy your life will suddenly feel less-important, and they will be replaced by other more important ones that deserve your attention.

One interesting piece of information that attracted my attention while I was conducting research for this chapter was the elevated rate of success of individuals working outside their native countries or comfort zones. These people were not continuously distracted by corruption or complications. So they take it easy and start achieving their objectives, unlike a local employee who spends too much time on planning and carefully studying all the complicated options before execution.

RULE #7 IN A NUTSHELL

ACT AS IF

Just close your eyes for a second and imagine that all of your loved ones suddenly vanished from your life... How would that feel?

The most important people, events, and materials in your life can be taken for granted when you start believing they will stay there forever without any effort from your end. But when you ACT AS IF they will vanish from your life the next day, you will start appreciating them more and exerting the right efforts towards them so you don't regret it later on.

One interesting experience which taught me a valuable lesson about efficiency happened as I was writing this book. As I reached my office which is considerably far from my house, I figured that I had forgotten my laptop charger back at home. It was 7:30 AM and I had a deadline at 11 AM and a laptop with a battery that would operate for a maximum of two hours. I needed to work around one more hour for my project to be finalized and uploaded. I realized that I couldn't waste a single second; I had exactly one hour to finish one full hours' worth of work. And I did it! And now, sometimes I act as if this situation is repeating itself.

So remember,
        Prioritize, and then ACT AS IF your life depended on it!

DON'T STOP TILL
YOU'VE DONE YOUR 20

A fter you've spent some time on Rules #5 & #7, you should now be familiar with goal-setting as well as long & short term prioritization models.

In this rule, we're going to get deeper into the present situation and what can/should be done in your present day. This rule is very simple.

The 80/20 rule

In 1906, an Italian economist, Vilfredo Pareto observed that 80% of the land in Italy was owned by 20% of the population. He also developed the principle by observing that 20% of the pea pods in his garden contained 80% of the peas.

Pareto's observation created what we call today the "80/20 rule" that made the rule of thumb in disciplines like mathematics and especially sales: "80% of your sales comes from 20% of your clients".

Now what does that mean for you?

It simply means that out of 10 Tasks that need to be performed on a daily basis, 2 of them are worth the entire 8 combined together.

Now I'd like to direct your attention towards the *20*. There are 2 theories here: The Common theory & the Treadmill theory.

1. The common theory is what was described before. It mainly focuses on tagging the AVAILABLE task, opportunity, client, etc… so all you have to do is to identify which one falls under the 20 tag.

2. The treadmill theory implies that in order to reach the rewarding 20%, you will have to fulfill the other 80% first, just like when working out on a treadmill. In a 1 hour exercise, your actual PEAK and the most rewarding segment is the last 12-15 minutes only. The first part is just a "warming-up" stage, but it is integral for you to rip the benefit of the 12 last minutes.

Don't STOP

To illustrate the core of this Rule, you need to visualize a scene from an action Movie where one of the bad guys is chasing and hunting down the good guys. I know it will sound weird, but try to follow with me on this.

The movie audience, in a way, admires the *persistence* of the bad guy in chasing the good guys. Nothing seems to stop him. He's always sharp and focused on his task.

For your best interest, you need to act like the above bad guy when dealing with your Top priority tasks, or actually your 20.

We all share the same 24 hours, and we all have more things to do than what we can in fact execute. The truth in which you should strongly believe is that you won't be able to do everything. So you will need to make sure you've done your top tasks with the most impact.

Once you've identified your 20, you should use Rule #7 and ACT as if you're going to take a 2 month-leave the next day. Ask yourself: which one of your 20% tasks needs to be done first?

Now the entire trick in this rule is just one thing: DON'T STOP till the task is done. *Keep your eye on the ball* and no matter what happens, you need to discipline yourself to finish the task. When you finish it, you directly start with the second task marked top priority; and so on until you have completed the TOP tasks of your day.

It is true that this is easier said than done, for many factors play a significant role in making this happen such as having the proper "mindset" at the time. But frankly, those same reasons would never disappear. So here are some compiled tips and tricks that would help you enhance your skills in that domain.

"Even if you are on the right track, you will get run over it you just sit there..."

~ Will Rogers

Guru Tips

- First, identify the time of the day when you're most productive; every one of us may have a different time when they are more productive. Some can be productive early morning, some in the afternoon and others even very late at night…

  It doesn't really matter which time of the day you're most productive; what really matters is that you need to know when that is, and schedule your 20s during that time. You can schedule the less important tasks to times when you know that your energy is lower. Let me give you an example of that:

  When I was still at Microsoft, I was constantly traveling, and there would be times when I needed to file my expenses. You have no idea how much I hated that task. I needed to scan the small receipts and fill in excel sheets… The task doesn't actually take more than 10 minutes, and it doesn't require too much thinking. But since I hated it, I always felt that it takes forever to be done. I used to schedule this task at the end of my very long days when my energy was very low and I didn't feel like "thinking". This feeling is common at the end of a day in the fasting season.

- Schedule some UN-Interrupted time for you to finish the most important tasks. During this time, you don't answer your phone or accept anyone to pass by your office. You make sure that Nothing stands between you and your 20s.

  In a 1:1 meeting with the operations manager in one of my companies, she was telling me that it's very hard for her to focus on finishing those important tasks because of the open space culture in the company where everyone feels invited to "interrupt". That was forcing her to stay late in the office to finish her tasks…

What I did was that I bought her a small battery-operated light, the same one used in emergencies or in camping. I told her to place it on her desk, and I sent a note to the whole office that if the Light was ON on her desk, then NO ONE and NOTHING is allowed to interrupt my employee.

She was required to schedule her un-interrupted time ahead because if the light were switched on all the time, it will lose is value and true meaning.

- Touch everything Once: this is SO important. We DON'T commonly use that when we view and process our emails. You open your email, scan it, then close it and continue to the next one and the next one. Later on, you'll go back to the one you viewed earlier to "see" if you're going to decide to work on it now or later. That alone is the source of wasting at least 25-30% of your time.
  So the rule of thumb here is to "Process" your items first, then you can actually Execute them. So you go through the papers in your Physical Inbox ONCE, and you take a decision concerning each of these papers immediately on the spot (check Rule#2 and apply the 4Ds in this case). Remember that once you scheduled a time to do it, you're done with that paper (or email) for now.

  I use this excessively in email communication, and I apply the David Allen "Getting Things Done" method and go beyond that with the McGhee applied method on Microsoft Outlook; so far I'm really happy with the results.

- Eat that Frog: let's face it: not all of the tasks we have to do on daily basis are tasks we "enjoy" doing. So the common thing that happens here is that we *Procrastinate* hoping that something would happen and we won't have to finish that task.

  Now I've read a lot on how to work around this "inconvenience", and I found the best description of the solution in the Guru Brian Tracy's *"Eat that Frog"* method.

Tracy brilliantly explained it in his books and programs (and I recommend you to experience them yourself because they are worth every second). He said that you need to imagine that you need to eat a LIVE Frog every day, and that live frog would be your most disgusting and annoying task of the day. So it doesn't really help to stare at it for too long. You need to finish with it as soon as you can and as quickly as you can, and afterwards you can rest assured that nothing worse can happen that day.

RULE #8 IN A NUTSHELL

DON'T STOP TILL YOU'VE DONE YOUR 20

Realize that not everything you're doing has the same weight and impact on what you're aiming to achieve.

The 80/20 rule is all about that 20% of the tasks you need to do, which are in fact worth the 80% of the tasks Left all together. So you need to identify which those 20% in your 100% are.

The Key afterwards is NOT TO STOP once you have started with the top task out of the 20% until it's Done; otherwise, you will risk not finishing it and getting overwhelmed with other less important tasks (and yes the *UGLIEST* tasks need to go *First*).

And remember,

Identify the tasks with the most impact and then Don't Stop until you're done with them… It's as simple as that!

USE TECHNOLOGY TO YOUR ADVANTAGE

aving been a "Technology Evangelist" for a long time (this was literally in my actual title at Microsoft), I have proudly had the chance to explore this beautiful world from different angles.

A few words on Technology evolution

In the customized sales seminars I give to technology companies, I always share with my audience slides that illustrate how technology has evolved.

There's nothing more frustrating for anyone who works professionally with technology than the *SPEED* of its evolution. Years of experience and learning can expire before your eyes, and you will have to start all over. The need to keep up with all the new software versions and features and even to anticipate what's going to come in future versions can really be a pain in the neck.

That's why I try to explain the evolution in a very simple way. The Evolution of technology is CLOSELY related to our *needs*; this means that every single upgrade is related to a need for someone or something.

So when you look at its evolution, focus on the needs the technology serves rather than on how the feature is developed. The bottom line of the evolution is that it was created to be *At Your Service*.

The following diagram can give you a simple idea of what I'm talking about.

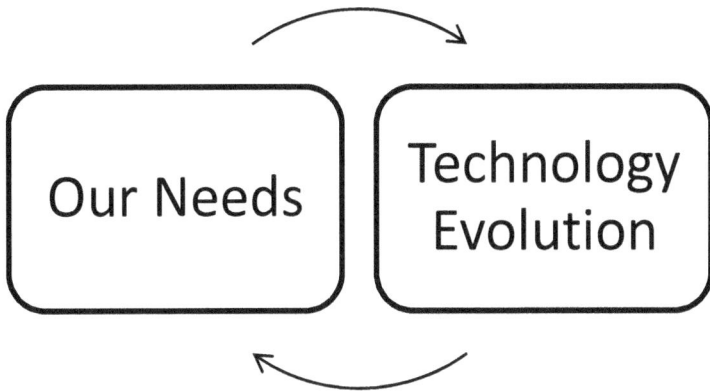

Technology evolution will continue to be driven by our needs and we will have new needs with every new evolution.

Technology Today

I have always said this, and will always say this again and again as it will always be true.

"Technology is MORE innovative and advanced today than it ever was before, and it won't stop progressing"

Back in the days when people started to realize the importance of technology, it was tightly linked to the word "Automation", from the beginning of the industrial revolution and up to our days. Technology was initially meant to SAVE OUR TIME and make us more productive.

If you look at the beautiful device that 60% of the world population holds today, *the mobile phone,* you will learn all you need to know about how technology evolved.

In 100s of lectures, I have given the example of how a 12-year old today would find it very hard to believe that there were days when the mobile phone was only used for its main purpose which is *just* to make and receive phone calls. There were no colors, no cameras, no mp3 players, no radios, no applications, no games, no calendars, no internet, no videos…

And just like you can't remember the days when you used to hang out with your friends without cell phones, and how hard that must have been, you can definitely watch the world today and see how businesses have evolved, and how many boundaries were broken which allowed international businesses to be brought to the local market.

So, it's important to highlight the importance of technology in our lives today, and how can we use it to make us more productive and to save our time.

Use Technology to your advantage

When you embrace that technology is part of your daily life and is no longer something to be afraid of, you can simply look at the bright side and see what it would offer to you.

The internet

On the internet for instance, you can find almost anything you are looking for by using Google or Bing; with the Auto-Complete feature, you will be amazed at how easy it has become to search without even fully & exactly "knowing" what you want in advance…

Online Videos

Back in 2002, in my home country Lebanon, we founded a group of technology enthusiasts made up of a community of individuals interested in a specific topic. We would share our experience about a technology or products, and we used to learn something new every month. The experience was excellent because it was a revolution compared to the old days when information was hard to find.

Today, you can virtually learn anything online; information is available everywhere. You can visit YouTube and search for anything, from playing the guitar to salsa dancing, editing movies, the new features of Microsoft office 2010 and the list go on and on and on…

Impressive! Isn't it!

You can seriously save loads of time by watching a video about whatever you need to learn. For instance, I was preparing to give a course on Supply Chain Management. Although I had good experience in the Technology aspect of the SCM, I needed to refresh my memory concerning what's going on in the world. So I found numerous videos that explain almost everything there is to know about Supply Chain Management from different sources, and I greatly refreshed my knowledge and learned 5-weeks' worth of information in as little as 2 hours.

Seriously, just pick virtually any topic you want to learn about, and look it up on YouTube. You can start seeing results in no time.

Remember that those 10 minutes you're going to spend there can save you hours and hours spent elsewhere.

Virtual Storage

When my older brother Maher got married and moved out of our parent's apartment, he was moving his stuff from our shared room. He kept on telling me to have a "Brave Heart" and throw away stuff that I'm not using anymore.

We collect lots of "Stuff" over the years, and we tend to keep everything even if we don't use them anymore. They are just THERE.

Now the rule of thumb here is that anything that you haven't used in 6 months must go… (With the exception of legal documents, etc…)

But this rule of thumb shouldn't be viable to use with virtual storage. Hard disks these days can store 1000s of times more than they could 10 years ago, with just a fraction of the price.

I still remember my brand new 486 computer, with 420 MB of hard disk storage and a CD-ROM that I bought for 1,000 USD; whereas now I can get an 8 GB USB Key for 29.99 USD and I can store in my pocket what was un-imaginable for me in 1993.

So don't throw away the documents & files you don't use; KEEP EVERYTHING… but keep them organized.

Today, I have all my email communications done in the past 10 years *stored & searchable* on my computer and even online using free email providers such as Hotmail, Gmail and Yahoo; you can access your email & documents from anywhere and search through them.

Communication to the Masses

Besides the obvious use of email communication, today's evolution of social networks such as Facebook and Twitter made it possible to communicate with the masses.

Once, I was talking to one of the most respected & influential technical community gurus, Scott Hanselman; he told me that he once heard a story that we all have a limited number of *Key Strokes*. So if you want to reply to questions, there's a limit on the number of how much you can type in your life. So instead of individually replying to each question, you can post the answer somewhere, and have the whole world see your answer.

So with every time you want to communicate anything to a large group of audience, BLOG it. This way, it will be searchable; it will stay there and you will see people from all over the world reading, commenting and interacting with you.

I also used to have difficulties keeping up with ALL my friends about all the things I'm doing in my life; but now thanks to Facebook & Twitter, I can have my strategy of "sharing" my news among friends, colleagues, clients and I can even interact with people I met when I was giving conferences all over the world.

So it's simple! You post one thought on Facebook and it's instantly available to 100s and even 1000s of people. (I highly recommend that you put a *strategy* on how to do that, especially concerning what you share. You should learn about privacy features in every website you want to use.)

My good friend Maher Al-Khayat, Marketing Manager at Microsoft Jordan, extended the usage of Twitter to his Out-of-Office reply. He states, *"I will be out of office x to y, so if you want to keep up with me you can follow my twitter @mkhay"*

And finally on social networking, using professional websites such as LinkedIn is almost essential these days. You can keep your professional CV up-to-date and one-click-downloadable from there. Your professional network will also be up-to-date, from co-workers and colleagues to partners and clients. You can even keep an updated profile of your company.

"The number one benefit of Information technology is that it empowers people to do what they want to do. It lets people be creative. It lets people be productive. It lets people learn things they didn't think they could learn before, and so in a sense it is all about potential"

~ Steve Ballmer

Manage your Time with Technology

First things first: physical notepads *won't cease to exist*. No matter how GREEN you want to go, being 100% digital is far away from being fulfilled. But there are lots of ways to save the environment by economizing your use of paper and using recycled materials, etc.

The main reason for this is that we write to concentrate our thoughts. So when you take notes in a meeting, and when you brainstorm by scribbling with your pen on a piece of paper, it's simply because this is the *right* way of concentrating.

Afterwards, the result of your written notes needs to be moved somewhere else.

I have seen lots of diaries as well as physical calendars and agendas here and there, used an abused by some and barely opened by others.

Now as much as people would love to have their Time Management tools looking very classy, stylish and corporate, the best tool in the world won't help if you don't use it properly. That's why I don't recommend you rely solely on physical calendars.

With the beginning of the use of PDAs (Personal Digital Assistant), more people are using the digital calendars to consolidate their appointments and have "BEEPY" Reminders.

But as of 2011, our to-do list and tasks come from lots of different sources, mainly from email communication, phone calls and meetings. Your to-do list has many dependencies (physical and electronic) saved elsewhere.

Following Rule #6 which says STOP USING YOUR HEAD, you will need a place to drop the To-Do reminders somewhere accessible, dependable and reliable.

Probably the best example to help illustrate the proper migration plan is the use of the Physical Address book and the migration to the Mobile phone.

At some points in the past, we used to separate the Phone Number from the email of the person. So, you had your contact's phone numbers stored on your phone or physical address book, and their email contact addresses stored on your computer. There were even times when you couldn't store more than one number for the same person so you had to duplicate contacts:

- On your Phone:
    - o   Samer Chidiac HOME
    - o   Samer Chidiac MOBILE
    - o   Samer Chidiac WORK

- On your Computer:
    - o   Samer Chidiac Hotmail
    - o   Samer Chidiac Corporate

You needed to look up and manage many contacts here and there...

And before the times when the "Sync-with-PC" even existed in the world of mobile phones, you would fear to lose all your contacts' information if you lost your phone, so you would duplicate the same data somewhere else.

Nowadays, technology makes life much easier. For me, by using Microsoft Outlook and having a corporate email account that uses Microsoft Exchange server, I have all my emails, contacts, calendar and tasks synchronized on all my PCs / Laptops / iPads as well as my mobile Phone. Instantly, whether using Wi-Fi or GPRS, everything is synched in all directions.

And guess what?   There is one entry for each contact that can includes multiple emails, multiple phone numbers and even birthdays & anniversaries. How easy is that?

So now, I don't worry about losing my contacts, calendar and life with a lost computer, lost phone, or lost tablet because I can get back into action in literally no time. And whether I create a new contact on Outlook or on the phone, I can add a new appointment from my phone, my iPad or Outlook; they are all synched in *Real-Time*.

Everything is stored on the hosted servers. This means that *the worst case scenario* for me that would result in losing all my contacts, emails tasks and calendar would be when all my devices crash or get lost: my mobile phone AND my computer AND my tablet / iPad AND the Datacenter 1000s of Miles away from me AND all their back-ups (which are normally stored in a different geographical location such as another State). I will lose my contacts only if a hurricane destroyed the world!

So chances of all this happening are slim.

That's why when you utilize technology mixed with your physical system, you can get peace of mind and be more productive.

And Outlook Tasks is a tremendous time-saver and consolidation. You can drag emails and documents and convert them to tasks, set categories, statuses, reminders and even assign tasks to others and follow up on them.

Everything is also Searchable!

Although my examples were mainly focused on Microsoft (you can easily tell why), Google, IBM, and Yahoo also provide almost identical productivity suits that sync with your computer, tablets and mobile phones; they are accessible directly from the Web.

RULE #9 IN A NUTSHELL

USE TECHNOLOGY TO YOUR ADVANTAGE

Do use technology in every way you can, because it existed and stayed to *SERVE* your needs.

Continuously look for best practices from the internet and save considerable time by watching online videos.

Do use the physical notebooks to put your thoughts together and take notes, but make sure to *summarize the info and put it on your* Computer.

And yes, *TRUST* the system you will use; this way, you will free your head. Use your mobile, laptop, tablet, pc, or anything that syncs to transfer your action point from your head to your electronic Tasks System.

YES... YOU CAN SAY NO!

Although I have studied Business Management and Computer Science when I was in college, my professional life started with more emphasis on the Technical & Programming part rather than the Business part…

If you're an engineer, a programmer, if you ever had or still have any technical role, you would definitely understand what I'm going to say next.

"I never learned to say NO to a task…"

For some reason, the mindset of a technical person is programmed in a way that as long as there's a light at the end of the tunnel, there's no need to say NO to a task.

And that, by the way, is not healthy because meeting expectations becomes more challenging when you need to execute something at a specific time and in a specific manner rather than to just finish it "eventually"…

So growing up with that mindset, I never learned to say NO; and I thought that it was just me, until I discovered that this "symptom" was more common than Facebook. There are a lot of people, technical and non-technical, who have difficulties saying NO.

It's funny that when you were two years old, that word was maybe the only word you actually enjoyed saying. And that's why they call that age "The Terrible Twos".

Well on many occasions, we *have* to say NO…

Saying NO to People

There are many people who would really exploit you and drain you.

- They can have negative influence.
- They de-motivate you.
- They take advantage of you & your kindness.
- They have the tendency to finish (or not) what they are doing and then come over to waste your time.

You must have met someone who fits the descriptions in the above list. And now, you should know what you should do.

YES... You can say NO!

You may have a colleague who needs a "favor" from you. He may want you to fill in his place while he goes out on a date. By doing so, you will be missing out on something you would love to do...

YES... You can say NO!

Your boss gives you a task that you know for sure you can't deliver unless you have to work unpaid overtime at the office or over the weekend. This will affect your work on other on-going projects you have to work on.

YES... You can say NO!

But be diplomatic! Don't just say no to everything, especially when you don't have a valid reason for that. On the other hand, use NO to re-negotiate a deadline or a specific Task.

For instance, if you have a project due August 1st and on July 20 you learn that you will not be able to deliver it on time; you should notify concerned parties as soon as possible. This way, you will have a better chance to re-negotiate the deadline instead of not being able to deliver at all or delivering poor quality work because of lack of time.

"Mastering the art of under promising and over delivering requires the ability to say no, when and how with conviction"

~ Thomas J. Powell

Another time waster are not people directly, but events…

Saying NO to Events

Events are any occurrences that can have direct or indirect interference in your work, from simple phone calls to serious accidents. Some events are totally beyond your direct control. You will have to deal with them; but the truth is that you do not need to deal directly with all the events that happen.

Interruptions fall in this category as well. You may be in the middle of an important task, and then you may feel the urge to just check your Facebook friends' updates. A song may suddenly occur to you and you may feel the urge to look it up on YouTube and listen to it.

You need to resist the *temptations* and SAY NO. Make a note instead to do that later on.

You're working on a task, and you over-hear a conversation about something. You feel that you need to drop everything and participate in the discussion.

One word: NO!

Saying NO to Opportunities

So far, we've learned to say NO to negative people, negative events and negative temptations, but what about Positive Opportunities?

This is the trickiest of all. You need to spend a considerable amount of time applying Rule #5 (Know where you're Going and why).

We always ask ourselves about the decisions we need to take when we are faced with opportunities because not every good opportunity is actually "Good", and not every "Bad" incident is actually bad.

It does take courage to say no to good opportunities; that's why I want to remind you of the example of "climbing a tree" from Rule #5.

When you're climbing a tree to reach to the top, it is very likely that the branches with the fruits are not on your way.

The same goes for good opportunities; they may not always contribute to the goal you've set or to WHERE you want to go.

The above example can be applied to BIG opportunities as well as small tasks. You may sometimes turn down more work or more overtime tasks when they stand between you and your time with your loved ones.

- Throw money at the problem and hire someone to do stuff for you!
- Throw money in exchange for time and say NO to tasks that would take away your time with your family

And in reference to Rule #3 when I discussed time management in Customer Service, saying no in a nice way can differentiate between an *excellent* waiter and a *regular* one. If you're at a restaurant and you ordered a specific meal and your order was delayed for one reason or another. A *regular* waiter would act normally and make you wait while an *excellent* waiter would simply apologize that your order might be delayed and offer you an alternative choice or some appetizer while you wait.

RULE #10 IN A NUTSHELL

YES... YOU CAN SAY NO!

I once watched a YouTube Video that shows Bill Gates & Warren Buffett giving a talk about the *Best Success Tips*.

Gates was talking to Buffett about getting together, so Buffett pulled his calendar and the pages were so BLANK. Gates was impressed and said "WOW, you've managed to avoid getting tied in to lots of kinda meaningless activities". So Buffett replied "YES you have to be good at Saying NO and picking the things that really make a difference".

Watching 2 LEGENDS talking about success made me realize that what matters the most is what's on your INNER-Scorecard rather than what's on your OUTER-Scorecards. Some people spend their whole time worrying about what others thought of them, wondering what the world thought about this and that. They did so instead of thinking about what *they* really thought of themselves and what they do.

Be *Assertive* in saying *No* to negative People; say *No* to events and temptations that would waste your time; Turn down good opportunities if they don't fall in the path of your "WHERE"; and in the end, exchange money for time especially if you have young children because you don't have ENOUGH time.

THE CONCLUSION

At this point, you surely realize that time-management is a vital skill. It impacts all the facets of your life, from your professional growth to your personal development. Yet, it is also important to realize that the Ten Unbreakable Rules of Time-Management are most effective when they are adopted as a lifestyle.

These Rules are to be perceived just like diets. Diets may work temporarily as people try to lose some weight over a couple of months. If the diet is not sustained and made into a lifestyle, the person is likely to regain the lost weight –and even more- and all his or her efforts would go in vain.

Similarly, when you adopt one or more of The Ten Unbreakable Rules of Time-Management, make it/them a habit. Applying one rule to solve a single problem may work in this particular situation, but making this rule a part of your life may prevent this problem –and many others- from happening in the first place.

ABOUT THE AUTHOR

SAMER CHIDIAC is internationally known for his unique methods in explaining very complicated business, technical & communication theories in very simple terms chosen from our day-to-day life.

He is the CEO of QUICK REFRESH, an Innovation Consulting Company. This book was based on the Successful Time Management Executive Refresher workshop delivered to Companies and Executives of different statuses and in different locations. Having an extensive experience in the Fast evolving world of Technology Marketing, Samer formerly worked for Microsoft Corporation as Technology Evangelist & Advisor.

Samer is also President of THINK COMMUNITY. Founded on the basis of effective time management, it is an international NGO that allows Individuals to effectively volunteer a portion of their Time on monthly basis to the benefit of the Community.

Samer is also the Winner of more than 7 local and International awards that include Microsoft Most Valuable Professional Award, Microsoft Customer Excellence Award, and the Best Mobile internet Business Model of 2002...

Also by Samer Chidiac: Work Love Balance: The Story of Adam; Work Love Balance: The Undercover CEO; Drive Your Way to MBA; The Power of You (a Revolution into Modern Advertising).

The full list of existing and future titles can be found at ChidiacBooks.com

.

www.ingramcontent.com/pod-product-compliance
Lightning Source LLC
Chambersburg PA
CBHW050512210326
41521CB00011B/2428